W9-BME-699

Hurray for Today!

I'm the Cat in the Hat
and I've called you both here
to celebrate holidays
all through the year.

The Cat in the Hat's Learning Library™ introduces beginning readers to basic non-fiction. If your child can read these lines, then he or she can begin to understand the fascinating world in which we live.

Learn to read. Read to learn.

This book comes from the home of

THE CAT IN THE HAT

RANDOM HOUSE, INC.

For a list of books in **The Cat in the Hat's Learning Library**, *see the back endpaper.*

The editors would like to thank
BARBARA KIEFER, Ph.D.,
Charlotte S. Huck Professor of Children's Literature,
The Ohio State University, and
TIMOTHY LLOYD, Executive Director, American Folklore Society,
for their assistance in the preparation of this book.

www.seussentennial.com

Library of Congress Cataloging-in-Publication Data
Worth, Bonnie.
Hurray for today! All about holidays / by Bonnie Worth ; illustrated by Aristides Ruiz — 1st ed.
   p.   cm. — (The Cat in the Hat's learning library)
SUMMARY: The Cat in the Hat explains the origins of various holidays throughout the year, some
well-known and some lesser-known, as well as some of the rituals associated with each.
ISBN 0-375-82275-5 (trade) — ISBN 0-375-92275-X (lib. bdg.)
1. Holidays—United States—Juvenile literature. [1. Holidays.]
I. Ruiz, Aristides, ill. II. Title. III. Series.
GT4803.W67 2004
394.26'0973—dc21
2003007404

Printed in the United States of America   First Edition   10 9 8 7 6 5 4 3 2 1

Hurray for Today!

by Bonnie Worth

illustrated by Aristides Ruiz and Joe Mathieu

The Cat in the Hat's Learning Library™

Random House 🏠 New York

I'm the Cat in the Hat
and I've called you both here
to celebrate holidays
all through the year.

So climb up on board
my new Party-Mobile,
where Party Thing One's
standing by at the wheel.

But before we take off
with the Bird of Katroo,
let's hear about holidays
from Party Thing Two.

Holidays are occasions
we have for a reason—
to mark someone's birthday
or ring in a season.

Each comes with a ritual.
What's that? you ask.
It's an action you take—
a joy or a task—

year in and year out,
either party or dance,
prayer or parade or
a series of chants,
that says a day's special
and worth more than a glance.

Dear Sally and Dick,
I can see you're perplexed.
How can we tell
one day from the next?

A thing called a calendar
shows us the way
to break up the year into
month, week, and day!
We live on one world
(and that is a fact),
but calendars differ
from this land to that.

Our 12-month calendar
says a year's done
when Earth has completed
one trip round the sun.

Seasons slice up our year
into four equal parts.
So let us begin
just before our year starts.

It's darker in wintertime.
Want to know why?
The sun does its shining
quite low in the sky.

On the first day of winter (which we call winter solstice), our part of the earth tilts away from the sun's kiss.

The old Romans tried
to make winter seem fun.

To make folks forget
they'd see less of the sun
and make up for the lack
of warmth and green leaves,
they lighted bonfires
and hung holly wreaths.

On winter fests now,
it is still quite the norm
to light up the darkness
and stay where it's warm.

On Christmas and Hanukkah
and dark Kwanzaa nights,
we hang wreaths, light up candles,
and string colored lights.

DECEMBER IS UNIVERSAL HUMAN RIGHTS MONTH!

The first day of January
what do I hear?
Folks making merry!
It's HAPPY NEW YEAR!

In the U.S. of A.,
minute one of month one,
we ring in the New Year
by having some fun.

Bidding bye to old habits,
we vow to improve
how we eat, how we dress,
how we look, how we move.

This vow to improve
(an age-old institution)
is known as a person's
New Year's resolution!

EAT RIGHT

HAPPY NEW YEAR

JANUARY IS NATIONAL HOBBY MONTH!

We know that the spring
cannot be far away
when we look at the calendar
and see Groundhog Day!

A groundhog who goes
by the moniker Phil
comes out of his hole.
Then this is the drill.

If his shadow this day
rises up clear and bright,
old winter will put up
a far longer fight.

If, instead, on this day
his shadow no-shows,
then Old Man Winter
just packs up and goes!

FEBRUARY is DENTAL HEALTH MONTH!

19

It's Valentine's Day!
Get your lips ready, dear,
for the smoochiest day
in the whole livelong year.

Valentine was a priest
who, during his life,
made sure that all lovers
could be man and wife.

They made him the saint
of all lovers. How fine!
A greeting card now
bears his name—valentine!

Their birthdays once came
as separate events.
Now one holiday
honors both presidents.

Can you guess
which great men
I am talking about?
If you know them,

don't whisper, just

let out a SHOUT!

DON'T FORGET
BLACK HISTORY MONTH!

21

A long time ago,
every Irishman knows,
snakes crawled over Ireland
(or so legend goes).

A great Irish person,
who called himself Pat,
drove out all the snakes—
and, by gosh, that was that!

22

Today we wear green.
It is our little way
to honor St. Patrick
on St. Patrick's Day!

Green stands for clover
(shamrocks, I've been told)
and for wee leprechauns,
who hide pots full of gold.

23

In March, spring begins
new life and rebirth!
Farmers and earthworms
start digging the earth.

To welcome the light,
we sing and we dance
and go on a picnic
and feed all the ants!

If you follow the arrow
to that little box,
Thing One will explain
about spring equinox!

Equinox is a word
meaning equal and night.
Half this day is in darkness
and half is in light.

Make way for NATIONAL MATH MONTH,
NATIONAL HISTORY MONTH, and
NATIONAL OCEAN MONTH, too.

I'll tell you a story,
which you might find funny,
about how the Easter fest
came by its bunny.

In jolly old England,
or so I have heard,
the goddess called Eastre
found a dying bird.

To save it, she changed
it—poof—into a hare!
Off that hare hopped then
without a hare care!

But in spite of its long
bunny ears and its legs,
this rabbit could still lay
a birdie's white eggs.

To thank the great goddess
for his life so new,
he painted his eggs
pink, yellow, and blue!

APRIL IS NATIONAL POETRY MONTH!

27

And where are we now?
Second Sunday in May,
which is much better known as
good old Mother's Day!

The day when we honor
our dear mother's worth
started out as a tribute
to great Mother Earth.

It was sort of like Earth Day,
only people would bake
a loaf out of fruit
called a mothering cake!

ATTENTION: MAY IS
NATIONAL PHYSICAL
FITNESS and SPORTS
MONTH

The very last Sunday
that happens in May,
we take time to honor
Memorial Day.

On Memorial Day, as
you may well have read,
we stop and we honor
our noble war dead.

We let our flag fly,
as you see, at half-mast
to honor those brave souls,
both present and past.

The first day of summer!
Hurray, summer's here! With
more hours of sun than
the rest of the year!

The days now are long.
They are hot and so sunny.
It's the best time to visit
a beehive for honey.

DON'T FORGET FATHER'S DAY!!!

And that is the reason
the full moon in June
is known by the
sticky-sweet name: honey moon!

No crops needing planting,
no frost threat to dread
makes summer the best
of all times to get wed!

HURRAY for FLAG DAY!

On the first day of summer
(we call summer solstice),
our part of the earth tilts
toward the sun's kiss.

EARTH

SUN

It's July the Fourth!
This grand day represents
the signing of the
Declaration of Independence!

By the King of England
we declared we would be
no longer ruled over—
yes! We would be free!

We march in parades
under bright stars and stripes.
We watch fireworks
of all colors and types.

JULY
IS
NATIONAL
PARKS
and
RECREATION
MONTH!

The Monday that's first to
come up in September
is the day we Americans
all pause to remember
hard-working workers
like cobblers, technicians,
carpenters, teachers,
cooks, and beauticians.

We pause to admire
the things they have made.
And Labor Day often
brings on a parade!

SEPTEMBER is LIBRARY CARD SIGN-UP MONTH!
SIGN UP NOW!
WHATEVER YOU DO, DON'T FORGET GRANDPARENTS' DAY!

Kick off your sandals.
Grab your wool socks!
The calendar reads
autumnal equinox.

By September 20
(sometimes 22),
the crops are all ripe and
the growth season's through.

The harvest is ready
to pick and to reap.
We pick some to eat.
We pick some to keep.

All through the ages
since those days of old,
we've thrown one last party
before it grows cold.

36

We feel kind of spooky.
Perhaps this is why:
the leaves now change colors,
then dry up and die.

NATIONAL FIRE PREVENTION WEEK happens in October.

Halloween is the party
where we are all hosts
to witches and vampires,
werewolves and ghosts.

Poor Jack was a bad man
who passed away, so
he went up to heaven.
But God told him, GO!

The devil did, too, so
he just walked the night.
A turnip was all that
he had for a light.

DID YOU KNOW THAT...

To Wandering Jack
of wee turnip-light fame,
today's jack-o'-lantern
just might owe its name.

... OCTOBER IS FAMILY HISTORY AWARENESS MONTH?

Late November brings us
the last—but not least—
party in this book,
the Thanksgiving feast!

We gather with family
and friends and join hands,
pray for peace and for plenty
in all the world's lands.

It's winter again and
what is this we're learning?
Our year's like our earth.
It just keeps on turning!

NATIONAL
CHILDREN'S BOOK
WEEK happens in
NOVEMBER

GLOSSARY

Beautician: A person trained to cut and style hair.

Chant: A short, simple song that is repeated, usually without musical instruments.

Honor: To pay high respect to someone or something.

Institution: A set law or custom or way of acting.

Moniker: A nickname.

Perplexed: Puzzled or confused about something.

Represent: To serve as a sign or symbol of.

Ritual: Something we do to mark a day as special.

FOR FURTHER READING

The First Thanksgiving by Linda Hayward, illustrated by James Watling (Random House, *Step into Reading*). Learn about the very first Thanksgiving in this exciting true story. For grades 1 and up.

The Fourth of July Story by Alice Dalgliesh, illustrated by Marie Nonnast (Aladdin Paperbacks). Find out more about America's birthday celebration. For preschool and up.

Holiday! Celebration Days Around the World by Deborah Chancellor (Dorling Kindersley, *DK Readers*). Read about special days all around the world. For grades 1 and up.

The Summer Solstice by Ellen Jackson, illustrated by Jan Davey Ellis (Millbrook Press). All about the importance of the summer solstice across time and cultures, including celebrations and legends. For grades 2 and up.

Valentine's Day by Gail Gibbons (Holiday House). Find out how we celebrate this fun holiday and learn its history. For preschool and up.

INDEX

The Cat in the Hat's Learning Library™

Fine Feathered Friends

A Great Day for Pup

Hurray for Today!

If I Ran the Rain Forest

Inside Your Outside!

Is a Camel a Mammal?

Oh Say Can You Say DI-NO-SAUR?

Oh Say Can You Say What's the Weather Today?

Oh Say Can You Seed?

Oh, the Things You Can Do That Are Good for You!

On Beyond Bugs!

There's a Map in My Lap!

There's No Place Like Space!

Wish for a Fish

Coming in Spring 2005:
Oh, the Pets You Can Get!